Musings
of the
Moment

A BOOK OF POEMS

CHARLES S. RIGBY

New Initiatives
Publications

Editing, typesetting, and cover design: Sally Hanan of Inksnatcher.com
Cover photo:.123rf.com/profile_alchena'>alchena /123RF Stock Photo
Author head shot: Lisa Cohan

Ordering Information:
Quantity sales. Special discounts are available on quantity purchases by corporations, associations, and others. For details, contact the author at the e-mail address above.

Musings of the Moment /Charles S. Rigby
ISBN 978-1-7321671-0-0

Dedicated to my wife, Ethel, and to all the people who have planted the seeds of experience in my life. I pray that this compilation of my thoughts might inspire you as they have inspired me.

To Fred

With Appreciation.
for being the Best
Plumber ever. —

Sincerely,
Chuck Rigby

CONTENTS

Letter from Charles

Writing is a spontaneous thing with me. I write from a heart filled with joy, hope, and anticipation. Having said that, my writing reflects my responses to places I have been and experiences I have had. Often after a meeting or when I have conversed with a person, I write a poem reflecting my impressions and responses to the experience. Other times I write in response to something I have read.

I believe that each poem has something that people can identify with as they reflect back over their life experiences. In this compilation are poems and lyrics to my songs that are my responses to things someone has said. At times throughout the book, I give introductory material to several of the poems. I hope that all of this will add depth to the meaning and expression.

Framing my thoughts poetically helps me use fewer words to explain the expressions of my heart. I hope it will also help you to look deeper than the writings and into the underlying principles that frame the prose.

Lastly, before you begin I want to ask for God's richest blessing on all the sowers and the harvesters who have been used to plant the seed in the ground that lies before you as you take the time to read the work.

Thank you,

Charles

Thoughtfulness

A warm and homey summer place,
Prepared for us as friends,
Gives warmth to hearts of countless guests
When summer finally ends.

For the comforts brought by your thoughtfulness,
For the love that's shown by your care,
For all you've been to so many folk,
In weather rain or fair.

To the best of years that lie ahead,
To the memories that remain from the past,
We thank you so much as to others we give,
Till heaven's reward comes at last.

On Ecology

We build a future
While polluting a stream,
For to build seems always right.
But the polluted stream
Holds the key to the end
Of the earnest builder's plight.

Love Comes Home

Love, a source beyond belief that
Emanates from the comprehensive soul
Of predetermined purpose.
Deep from the foundation of sovereign essence
Comes the surge of power unfolding in our hearts,
Motivating our desire to reach out and touch
The lives of others.
Love, this indefinable inherent attribute exudes
An energy that conquers hate
Where hate can never conquer love.
The insatiable appetite of love serves to
Energize the drive of human expression
Among our fellow peers,
But finds itself a pittance
When one considers God the source of all.

Happy Birthday

We wish you happy birthday
It's a special day for you.
We hope you have the best of times
With friends and family too.
May every day that follows
Be filled with love and cheer.
We hope to see you back again
To celebrate next year.
Happy Birthday to you.

Savor the Moment

Savor the moment, each moment you live.
Be sure of yourself and to others give.
Remember the moment that passed you by.
Learn from past deeds that have made you cry.

Savor the moment, the one that's just now.
Pray to God that he'll show you how.
Don't take for granted the time that you have.
Treat every moment like a healing salve.

Savor the moment you spend with a friend.
Hope that its essence never will end.
Strive for the moment you celebrate love.
Do it with guidance that comes from above.

Savor the moment as you reach for the top.
Hold on to your values and don't let them drop.
Remember the moments that you have lost.
Those moments of waste have a precious cost.

Savor the moment; remember the past.
Invest in the future with things that will last.
But build in the present, make certain the way.
Your reward will be there at the end of the day.

When Loved Ones Die

Waves of grief well up within,
Spilling over through tear ducts
Onto the pillow of despair.
To whom shall one turn
When overwhelmed with anguish and loss?

We lose control of destiny through death
That crashes into our lives without a moment's notice.
With disregard and disrespect for schedules of others
And plans already made.

It reigns for a moment.
Its lingering loneliness subsides
Only to smash upon us again and again,
Reminding us of how fragile a course
The journey through life really is.

How dependent we are on the breath of God
For every action we take and every plan we make.
We are indeed linked to eternity
And anchored to earth

Only by the breath and spirit
That empowers our lives
And fills us with the consciousness
Of our dependence
On the permissive will of God.

Journey Run

The journey traveled on the road of life
Is often filled with struggles and strife.
It's the end of the race that counts the best,
The rest of the race is only a test.

If one would think that it's all in the run,
Then running would be all that lasts when it's done.
But follow the markers and surge toward the goal,
For it stretches resolve and takes its toll.

Run with great passion with the end in mind.
Press toward the mark; stay in front, not behind.
When at the last you've finished the race,
Make sure you've run it with mercy and grace.

Keep your eyes on the prize as forward you go.
Don't be distracted by each passing show.
Stay focused ahead for that home in the sky
That God has prepared in the "sweet by and by."

"Do you not know that in a race all the runners run,
but only one gets the prize? Run in such a way as to
get the prize" (1 Cor. 9:24). "I press on toward the
goal to win the prize for which God has called me
heavenward in Christ Jesus" (Phil. 3:14).

Pondering the Journey

Where do I focus my eyes?
Where do I plant my feet?
What do I allow my ears to hear
As I walk along life's street?

How do I stand in a dark place?
How do I push against the tide?
How do the foundations of my life
Keep me where I should abide?

When will I know the answer?
When will I cross the goal?
When will the impact of life's long road
Give assurance that anchors my soul?

What counts as meaning in life?
What should a valued course be?
Where will I stand when the wind blows strong
And resists the truth that I see.

Frenetic Thought

Emancipated to the frenzy
Of the urban undertow
That flails away in every way,
No matter where we go.

A stalwart, forceful, forward bent
It takes to beat the pressured fray,
To stand against the wayward press
And fight again another day.

Tough the stance it takes to see
The obstacles that loom so large,
To dodge the roughshod counterparts,
Protect our lives, and stay in charge.

At the weary end of day
When life is spent and work is done,
We tally up the hard-fought race,
And with confidence, we hope we've won.

Brush of Mind

A thousand plunging open thoughts
Surround my mind each day.
They bathe my life in vivid dreams,
Each one with things to say.

They probe the castle of my soul
And test its strong-built size.
They beat against the values held
That dwell in watchful eyes.

This rigid castle of my soul
Stands firm against the storm
That threatens peace within its walls
And comes to change its form.

They test the virtues of the best,
The better or the good.
They sometimes change the course of strength
From where the best had stood.

Ever watchful, ever strong,
I welcome living thought
To build upon the best of things
That life to me has brought.

Father, Forgive Them

Father, forgive them
For they know not what they do.
That was the prayer
From the cross for me and you.

Because he gave of himself
Upon the cross that day,
He opened for us
A new and living way.

Because he took his blood that was shed
And sprinkled it on the mercy seat,
He gave his life in suffering
With nail-pierced hands and feet.

We all should stop and ponder
What our response should be
To God's redeeming work that day
And what he did for you and me.

He made the full provision
And paid it all in love.
Our faith in his redeeming work
Assures our life above.

Reflecting Back on Bethlehem

Reflecting back on Bethlehem,
The city of his birth,
Thoughts give way to light and hope
He brought to human worth.
As he began life's awesome journey
On that first Christmas day,
His presence spreads throughout the world
To show us all the way.

The glory of God shines forth
Into the night of pain.
The gift of God is light and life
To all who seek the gain.
The grace of God is sufficient
For inclusion of the world.
From the manger to the cross,
His freedom is unfurled.

The Savior came and gave himself
For all the human race.
He taught and modeled service
In the fullness of his grace.

He walked the road with others,
Broke bread and kicked the dust.
He talked and as the living Word
Encouraged faith and trust.

Two thousand years of history
Have passed and still it stands.
The work of Christ has spread
Throughout the lands.

The world began to change,
When his glory pierced the night.
And from his living active Word
We walk in fellowship and light.

This Holy Place

The Lord is in this holy place.
We're thankful for this hour.
We bow our heads and join our hearts,
And seek his unifying power.

The Lord is in this holy place.
We're thankful for his saving grace.
Lord, join our hearts in unity,
Forgive our sin and set us free.

We sing as those redeemed,
We join as one in thee.
We celebrate in lasting hope,
The work of Christ that sets us free.

The Lord is in this holy place.
Let the people of the earth respond.
Our hearts are full of love's embrace,
With hope and grace for what's beyond.

Oh sanctify this worship hour.
May your presence with us reign.
Fill us with the Spirit's power
In earthly loss and heaven's gain.

The Lord is in this holy place.
We join in joyful song.
We lift our voices up in praise to him
In whom we are made strong.

Oh sanctify this worship hour,
May your presence with us be.
Until someday we leave this earth,
And spend eternity with thee.

Heading for Heaven

If you want to have hope
And you want to have faith,
If you want to go to heaven someday,
You've got to stop and open up your heart,
For Jesus is the only way.

You can't go to heaven on your wheels,
You can't buy your way through the gate.
You've got to get ready for the time is now,
'Cause you never know when it's too late.

God is there with compassion and care.
He's waiting outside the door.
He's waiting for you at the other side
As he always has been there before.

Adam pushed him away on that dreadful day,
And darkness took up the space,
But through his Son that he sent to die,
He shines on the whole human race.

God's waiting outside the door.
He's standing and waiting for you.
His purpose is clear, so be of good cheer;
He's waiting to carry you through.

Busy Worker

I'm busy, so busy in
The work of God.
Don't bother me with
The work of the sod.

I'll drop a word,
Just a word for you.
Water it with prayer
And it will come true.

"Pray through brothers"
And "God bless you!"
Say, "Praise the Lord"
To all you do.

Do busy workers think of others
Or only what they say?
Do they ever stop to give some thought
To the other person's way?

Take heed, you busy worker.
God not only talks to you.
His Spirit leads and also guides
The lives of others too.

Captured Moments

I've never passed this way before
And never will again.
For things will never be the same
No matter where or when.

It's only in this moment
That life is given to me.
A moment given only once
To which my soul is free.

The presence of this present state,
Yes given only once.
As moments add to hours,
Then weeks build into months.

Moments are but vessels
Available to you.
Their worth is made or lost
Upon the things we do.

For doing fills these vessels
As we use this world of now.
Let's pray that God of heaven
Will always show us how.

The Lighthouse Evermore

Hello, hello, hello, hello
Up and down the coast.
The lights of the lighthouses along the shore
Wake up to their evening toast.

They say hello to the sunset,
They wave to the stars in the sky,
They look out to the sea for every ship
That may go passing by.

As the darkness rolls in and night grows stern,
As the waves dash up all the more,
The light of the lighthouse beams its light
To protect ships from the rocks on the shore.

All through the night in the fog and the storm,
The light guides the way down the coast.
Only God knows how many are saved
By the light that shines from its post.

When night has ended and dawn comes at last,
The lights say goodnight for the day.
The sun takes its place in the sky above
And continues to show the way.

Those who are saved by the light of the night
Seldom think of the price that is paid
To shine out to them upon the ships,
Giving answers to those who have prayed.

But they have been there and always will be.
Just look on the rocks by the shore.
The lighthouse continues to send out the light
And is faithfully there evermore.

Hello, hello, hello, hello.
Night has come again,
And up and down the shores of hope
Are the lights that tell you when.

A New Day Is Dawning

At the dawn of each day
As the gospel light rings true,
Let the message of redeeming love
Shine out in all you do.

Be faithful to the message.
May our lives spread forth the Word.
Sow the seed of righteousness.
Serve with passion for our Lord.

Never falter in our purpose.
Lift up Christ the King of Kings.
Go with gladness, joy, and victory,
Knowing what salvation brings.

Send forth the light to every land,
Let it flow from shore to shore.
Until the Savior comes at last
To take us home forevermore.

Chorus
Oh a new day is dawning.
Speed the gospel to the world.
Send the truth by every means.
Let the banners be unfurled.

A Moment from God

I straddle an abyss
Between hit and miss.
I stand on the threshold of time.
At three score and four,
I stand at the door
And wonder what destiny's mine.

Will God turn and speak
Or is he marching ahead,
So busy in paving the way
To realize I've faltered
A step or two back
And need to feel his hand today?

I am wondering now
What I should do
To get back onto the trail.
It just seems to me
God should always be there
And never let his children fail.

Perhaps tomorrow
I'll hear his call
And catch the pulse of his voice.
And once again
I'll stand straight and tall
And know that I am his choice.

What's in a Prayer?

Have you ever stopped to think when you pray
As to how you would respond if you were
On the other end of your request?

Often we throw our prayers up there
In hope that someone will answer.
We offer up the most extensive list
Of undoable expressions and personal desires,
While giving little consideration as to how
We would respond if we were answered.

The doable, you-able exposition
Of dishing and dissing pours out of our souls
In our attempt to manipulate sovereignty
According to our personal goals.

When in our desire to stake out our turf,
Do we stop and realize that at all times
We stand in the presence of God
Who already knows and cares about our need?

God is patiently waiting for us
To realize we can't make heaven alone.
He is ready to help us and guide us
With directions which can reassure us
That someday we will meet him, and he will then
Point us toward the place he has prepared for us,
At home with him in heaven.

Shine Like the Stars

You shall shine like the stars in the heavens
Holding forth the full Word of life,
Blameless and pure in a troubled world
That is filled with darkness and strife.

You will lift up your hearts with assurance
That Jesus will carry you through,
Claiming the power of God's wondrous love,
His witness in all that you do.

Love for the purpose of what is right
By seeking God's strength to believe,
Walking tall through the storms of life,
Embracing his call to receive.

Chorus
You shall shine as stars in the heavens above.
You shall shine as the children of God's love.
Shine, O you children, keep on walking in the way.
Shine on, O you children, you're the people of the day.

Coda

Shine on, O you children; keep on walking in the light.
Shine on, O you children, like the stars in the night.
Shine like the stars in the night.
Shine like the stars in the night.

Text based on Philippians 2:15

Second Thoughts

Flat upon my back I lie
In solemn consternation,
My haste laid bare in crashing waste
Of real life's obligation.

It looms before my wanton face,
A vivid painful glare,
And only now I realize life,
Its meaning and its care.

I had a charge, I let it slip,
And now it's gone forever.
Yet it seems a while ago
Indeed that I was clever.

Oh, to have those moments back,
To give them back to others.
I'd plan a thoughtful, careful race
Without the loss of brothers.

In giving to another life
And seeing it grow strong.
I find reward for both of us
That works for lesser wrong.

When life is spent and shared with none,
When mine and mine alone,
I only find that loneliness
Is all I really own.

But concern that's spent for others
Is time with no limits set.
And as what's spent comes rolling back,
All life gets better yet.

For what if life is spent
And all the world is gained?
I only find a lonely heart
With a soul that's fully drained.

Repair is not the answer
To the scars of a life's vignette.
I know that a carefully committed heart
Brings peace and not regret.

Holiday of Love

The streets are aglow with the moonlight.
The roof glistens brightly with snow.
The trees are reflecting the season.
The bells are announcing the show.

Chorus
I'm looking for love this holiday,
I'm filled with hope and delight.
May our wish for this Christmas be
Happiness, and may his peace on
Earth be made right!

The parents are making things ready.
The kids all are singing the song.
The stockings are placed by the fireside,
And Santa will soon be along.

Chorus
I'm looking for love this holiday,
I'm filled with hope and delight.
May our wish for this Christmas be
Happiness, and may his peace on
Earth be made right!

Turn On the Lights

Turn on the lights, we're living in the day.
Turn on the lights, oh what can we say.
Turn on the lights, seek the things that are true.
Turn on the lights, it all begins with you.

The good life starts with an attitude.
The good life starts with you.
You pick the good life by making the choice
Of what you will give yourself to.

Just light a little lighthouse where you are.
You might be just a candle or a falling star.
The people all around you can't see so very far,
So light a little lighthouse where you are.

We've found the glow of happiness.
We've struck a light to light our way.
All gloom is gone and hope is here;
We're living in the day.

Remember love and friendship.
They're both not very far.
Reach out and help your neighbor.
Be a lighthouse where you are.

Looking for Love

The energy of love flows from my heart's desire
As I reach out in hope on pathways that inspire.
My eyes scan skies with notions from the start,
To seek a world of love that sets my life apart.

The heart that never finds the pulse of love,
Or beats a sacred song of intimate return,
Has never found the full release of life
And what it means to be beyond the yearn.

The boundless drift of one
Whose love is not yet found;
A wanderer who finds not a peaceful place
Cries out, "Oh where does happiness in love abound?"

It's there! It's there! Not far away,
Like a feeding mother at the end of the day.
That massive search of one great love I hope to find
In prayer I trust, when found, that love to me is kind.

Of Love

How would you like to sing a new song?
How would you like to be free?
How would you like to see for yourself
The love that's been given to me?

I'll show you that love, if you'll let me.
I'll try to give myself to you.
I'll be to your hopes what you can't see in dreams
And try to make love dreams come true.

You see a real dream lies a distance away
From being what real life can share.
But a dream is a hope that sets an ideal
That reality seldom can bear.

To give you my love, I hold on to you
And be to you all that I dare.
When all of our dreams and realities meet,
My love only hopes you will care.

Becoming

The value of the day
In this jar of clay
Is a wonder of nature's decree.

To capture a life
And transcend its strife,
One must take every breath that is free.

The constants we share
And the things we declare
Compile the essence of who.

At the end of the road,
When you've carried the load,
Your faith will determine the you.

Not Smart

A stupid thing to count on self
In fields I do not know.

It's only sane to find a guide
To show me where to go.

Just Beyond

I slipped on through to the other side,
In human terms, they say I died.

But the presence of God is a blissful place
That transcends all of time and space.

How I got here, I cannot explain.
I only know I'm not the same.

I'm now in a place where come to rest
All of the dreams and hopes of the best.

Just a moment passed as time faded away,
And here I stand in heaven's day.

Frozen Mind

Dogmatism is a euphemism
Of an inflexible mind.
The essence of decided state
A quirk of dense mankind.

Goodbye Song

We know we'll miss you always
As we say goodbye again.
We'd love to see you in tomorrow
Somewhere; we wonder when.

Don't frown about our parting,
We just love to see you smile.
We plan to see you sometime
Down the road of life awhile.

We know that parting's such sweet sorrow,
But it's joy we're after here.
And we know because we've met you
That we've shared both love and cheer.

So we say goodbye to friend,
And someday we wonder when
We will meet you,
When tomorrow is today again.

Kenosis

Let his mind be in you
As you set your sights on Christ alone,
He who took on human form
And through his death did sin atone.

Emptied of his grand esteem,
He put himself aside.
Humbled in his human state,
Upon a wretched cross he died.

God lifted him up to life again,
He set his name on high.
Jesus, the name above all names,
Was raised from death into the sky.

At the name of Jesus, every knee will bow.
Every tongue will confess his name.
To the glory of the Father, through the Son,
Things will never be the same.

Say That Again

With all the discourse in a world undone,
With all the passing of the blame,
With all the clamor for more of love,
There is more attraction found in human fame.

So as we shop our way through life,
Choosing what we believe and who will be our mate,
Select well the path that you will walk
And the decisions you will make.

There's a River

There's a river that flows forth from heaven.
Through love it has captured my heart.
Christ came to earth to set us free.
From his presence I'll never depart.

I want to live with heaven in mind;
I look for a city on high
Where no tears are shed and death is no more,
And we shine like the stars in the sky.

Flowing forth from the river of life
Is the power to live each day.
I seek the touch of the Master's hand
To guide me each step of the way.

Oh, there's a river, yes, a river
That flows from God's dear hand.
Coming down to earth from the source of life,
It travels across the land.

Oh, there's a river, yes, a river
That I drink from every day.
And it's from that living source of life
That truth comes to show me the way.

May Love Return Again

The eyes that search for a kindred smile each day,
The heart that longs for a love to come its way,
The path that's filled with longing hope sincere,
The face that's stained with sorrow from the tear.

They will rise with joy the day they see
Their one true love return to set them free.

The piercing darkness keeps them from the view
That once they had within the sphere they knew.
That tender touch and mortal grasp of gain
Was lost when love did fail in truth and brought them
pain.

But they shall rise with joy the day they see
That one true love return to set them free.

They're looking for tomorrow
With a rainbow in the sky.
They're searching every cloud
That may be passing by.

They know that through their prism of despair,
They'll someday find that source of love and care.

Yes, they will then rejoice the day they see
Their one true love return to set them free.

Revelation Rejoice

Chorus
Hallelujah to the Victor,
Hallelujah to the Lamb,
Hallelujah to the Christ we serve,
Hallelujah to the great I Am.

Salvation and full glory
To him who stands so true.
Just are the judgments of our God
On all that people do.

He keeps his every promise
With power through and through.
He condemns the evil ones on earth
And pays all sin its due.

He avenged the blood of servants
That served him to the end.
To the victors go the honored place,
From Christ to faithful friend.

Praise him all you servants,
Come forth both great and small
With faithful voice and willing heart.
Answer now the Savior's call.

For mighty is the King of Kings,
Rejoice, rejoice be glad.
Come join the wedding of the Lamb.
Lift up your hearts and not be sad.

Fine linen, bright and clean,
Ready dressed with righteous light,
We've come as bride forever
To Christ who conquered night.

A testimony of the saints,
In faithfulness we stand.
We've come as agents of his grace,
With love and hope and hand in hand.

Hallelujah to the Victor,
Hallelujah to the Lamb,
Hallelujah to the Christ we serve,
Hallelujah to the great I Am!

When God Spoke into Flesh

Highly favored in the plan of God,
Mary gave of herself to the end.
With wonder and fear in her innermost thoughts,
She served as mother and friend.

The day that Mary birthed God's Son,
The path to victory over sin was won.
The Word made flesh in servant's form,
Led to conquered death and change of norm.

The birth of Christ let it be known
He would one day sit on David's throne.
Above the turmoil in that glorious hour,
He infused the world with redemption's power.

Shocked

Shocked by the shallow discourse,
When all around us float the seeds of despair.
Escaping all the reality of responsibility
That all without exception should share.

Buyer beware! resounds the warning
Like a lighthouse shining on a stormy night.
Make decisions with eternal value
Based on principles of truth and right.

He's on His Way

I'm standing on the promises,
Waiting for the King.
I'm serving in his righteous love
That allows my soul to sing.

Gone are the days of despair.
Gone is the darkness of night.
Before me is a path of hope,
Full of assurance and light.

I'm looking each day for his coming,
For Jesus is coming again.
It's up to us to be ready,
For no one knows just when.

Why the Wait

Why can't we start out mature
For all the days of life we must endure?
Why can't we just be there?
Without the fuss of pain and toil and care?

Why can't we know from the start
Our role on the stage of life, our part?
Why can't we be there now
Without the need of those to show us how?

If we were there before we start,
Would we appreciate another's heart?
Growing up is fun to do
If you let the love of others lead you through.

Life is not about getting there.
It's about the journey on the way.
Growing step-by-step along the path of life
And finding each experience flow deeper every day.

When we reach our final goal
And understand at last what makes us whole,
When we look back upon the journey past,
May we who trust in God find peace at last.

Birthdays Happen

When birthdays roll around
At the turning of each year.
We stop, give thanks, and hug our friends
And give a hearty cheer.

The years go by; time marches on,
No matter what they say.
You trade your life for something
With every passing day.

So stop and think about your life
As you trek through trails untold.
Enjoy yourself and choose the best,
For all of us grow old.

That Passing Cloud

The ocean breakers rolled and foamed
Upon the open land,
While people lay in summer heat
And the sun beat down on sand.

The grains' expanse, I could not count
As I looked toward the sky.
I pondered dreams beyond my mind
As a cloud came rolling by.

The summer sun seemed dimmed by cloud
Its strength held from my view.
A cloud, a wondering lonely cloud
Kept the sun from shining through.

That's the way life is, I guess.
When the infinite shines its best,
A wandering cloud of finite stance
Makes us falter at life's test.

Ode to the Statue of Liberty

I stood in awe as I looked toward the sky
At that prodigious conglomerate of steel.
It's there alone, both day and night
As a symbol of all that I feel.

Amassed around with water,
It stands alone with me.
Then it rises up from earth
For all mankind to see.

Do we rub its rails and wear its stairs
Without the feel of pain?
Do we stand before its shadow
And do not know its reign?

A pauper dwarfed by its symbolled stance,
It stands for man made free.
Beyond oneself, its colossal voice
Rings out for liberty.

O symbol great, you are but there
To remind me what I am.
How far I've fallen from the mark
As a selfish, mortal man.

How'd I Miss It?

It passed me by and I'm not sure
If it was something I did, or something I said.
It seems like every time I look,
Life is filled with the stuff that I dread.

The fastidious notion of thinking thoughts
That are important enough to say,
Then having them delayed so long
To put them off for another day.

The squeaky axle gets the grease
Is often where we land.
It seems the one who causes fuss
Gets attention from the band.

It's the one who carves the turkey.
It's the voice that fills the air.
It's the one who dominates the scene
And never seems to care.

And all around that loud proclaim
Are those who seek to share
A piece of wisdom, thought, or deed
With candid poise and flair.

When will it be the time to speak
With clear and zealous voice?
Somewhere out there a moment waits
When you'll become the better choice.

Random Thoughts
of
Reasons End

Why not crush each stem of faith
That might pop up and flower?
Why not stomp upon the ground
From which you're shaped and given power?

Why not curse all reasoned thought
That offers peace and hope within?
Why not kill all thoughts that point
To some existing sin?

Why stand and judge
All those who stab the dark
With phony swords of light
That pierce the blinding stark?

Why not take the burden on ourselves
To reason away the truth
And put all faith upon a shelf?

Why not close the door
To the potential of grace?
Why not let our self-ideologue
Of reason set our pace?

Why not turn your eyes away
From prospects that are born of God?
Why not realize that God himself
Has walked upon this sod?

Lift Up the Message

Lift up the message
So clear and bold and true.
Share it with the dying world,
Reflecting Christ in all you do.

Make the message live.
May your life speak as your voice.
Proclaim the precious love of Jesus
Through every act and choice.

Let the Holy Spirit guide you
As you live each passing day.
Let the mind of Christ be in you
As you walk the sacred way.

It's the living active Word,
A light for all to see,
So you can say
Through grace and love,
Jesus only, Christ in me.

Chorus
Lift up the message
Jesus only, Christ in you.
Lift up the message,
And he will see you through.
Lift up the message
During every passing day.
Lift up the message
As you walk the sacred way.

Thinking of You

I thought I'd catch a bird,
I almost had it in my hand.
Then it slipped away from me.
Where will it go; where will it land?

It flies so high beyond my grasp.
Oh, to be so tall,
To have the wings with strength of flight
And never need to fall.

Above the trees, against the breeze,
Reflected toward the sky,
I see it go; it moves me so,
The soul that flies so high.

Aloft beyond the finite grasp
Gone now in ebbing day.
The flying soul moves out of sight
And darkness dims my way.

I stand and look and linger on
In hope for some return.
But gone it is, this bird of love
My heart so wants to yearn.

The love that's spent, is fading,
And now I must move on.
To find a fresh object of hope
To build my dreams upon.

Lost Hope

The beauty of a memory
In the guarded garden of pain.
The stalwart brave resolve
Of animated care and gain.

That afterglow that turned to tears
And darkens with the passing day.
Tears at the heart, the mind, the soul
And will not go away.

Is there light before the night,
I try to brush the shadows from my eyes.
My anguish pressed beneath the burden
Of the never-ending cries.

Down, down I go beneath
The surface of sustaining hope.
I fade each day
From all capacity to cope.

And there it ends! It's gone!
I've lost the strength to live.
Sorry bright future,
But your loss is all that's left to give.

In the darkest moment of despair,
When void of hope one loses sight of those who care.

Among the flowers and respect of peers,
The blindness caused by wretched pain and tears

That turns one down a road of no return,
And leaves behind the others who would yearn.

Oh, wasted future, gone with sudden blast
That bank of full potential downed so fast.

Gone! Alas, to earth forevermore in pain.
Continue on, you others, for it's only in your memory
That we'll ever meet again.

The Athlete

The fast-flowing fervor
Of infinitesimal fortitude
That exudes the determined effort
Of what practice should include.

It takes a race of hard demand
That goes beyond the goal,
A push that far exceeds the pace
Of the average mortal soul.

The conquest of a winner,
A thousand practiced days,
A triumphant victor's moment
Brought home with lauded praise.

Wanderings

I traveled along a fencerow
And came to an open gate.
I started down a lonely path
With time that couldn't wait.

I stumbled on the darkened way
That never saw my steps before
And wondered if, in loneliness,
I should have looked at life once more.

Is there a way that's brighter?
Is life just a game of chance?
Or is there more to life's road's choice
Than comes from just a glance.

The Christian says there is
A master to life's way,
Who fills a lonely, searching heart
With peace for every day.

Vacation Time

Once a year, we pack up our gear
And on to vacation we go.
We talk and we pray,
We swim and we play,
With all of the friends that we know.

Along the way
We stop for a day,
To savor a moment or two.
The day was so clear,
We gave out a cheer,
Vacation's a good thing to do.

When it's time to come back
We restuff our pack,
And return once again to the fuss.
Many blessings we share
With love and great care,
T'was good to be there with just us.

The Someone Who Cares

I read your letter
The other day.
I thought for a moment
And stopped to pray.

The sweetness of joy
From one who will care
Burst forth like a rose
In the summer air.

The essence of those
Who bridge life's concerns
Gives quality strength
To all that life earns.

The Lord calls us out
To walk in his way,
But your witness in life
Has brightened my day.

A City's Ways

I stood and looked at the skyline
On a bright and crisp fall night.
The wind murmured down through the buildings
And hauntingly told of the plight.

A world caught up in a cloud of dust
And pressed to a point of despair.
What reason, I thought, must the world be this way?
Is it only that God isn't there?

But there is a God, and he does have a part
In filling the vacuum of life.
But getting this God to the hearts of mankind
Is like lighting the darkness of night.

He's ready, it seems, to answer the call
Of a destitute, fast-failing world.
But could it be us who have failed at the helm,
And into a vacuum been hurled?

If God's always there—then where are you
When the many paths fall at your feet?
Perhaps only in God does it all come true,
For it's only in him we're complete.

Ever Love

The days were so dreary,
The nights were so long,
Time flew by me
While I stood alone.

Please help me. I call you.
Can I ever forget
When all that I love you with
Still loves you yet?

Abiding Strength

Lord, give me staying power
And give me grace,
That I may take a rightful stand
And find my proper place.

Lord, give me staying power
For a world that's full of need,
That I may flow with strength
For those we're sent to feed.

Lord, give me staying power
To keep me when alone,
And guide me on a straightened path
That by your love is shown.

Lord, give me staying power
That keeps me in the way,
And shows the path of properness
To live from day to day.

Lord, give me staying power
As I journey here in life,
With a wise and gentle touch
Amidst this world of strife.

Lord, give me staying power
Eternal and complete,
Until my life transcends this flesh
And walks on heaven's street.

He's Waiting for You

Come, calls the Savior.
Believe in me.
You left me for selfishness.
You couldn't see.

You only found loneliness
And need more than friend.
You search for the love
That my Spirit can send.

I reach out to you
Wondering why
Your heart will not share
When I ask you to try.

Oh, lift up and smile.
Oh, look up and see.
In the essence of love
Once paid to set you free.

Once more I ask you,
"Will you receive?"
I've given my life
That you may believe.

Accept me as Savior
For life made anew,
And then by My grace,
You'll see that it's true.

Sorting Ways

Sorting through the ways of life
That man presents to me
I search for one that satisfies
And makes my spirit free.

They say there are goals and roads to take,
Journeys built through time;
The question always in my soul
Is finding one that's mine.

Should I search for roads beyond the ones
Man's thoughts are prone to make,
Or choose a path that's ready made
And many people take.

I've heard there's one that goes beyond
The ways that oft seem right.
A narrow way, a challenged race
That shines with constant light.

A way that's shown from God above,
A way that starts with soul,
A way that takes my scattered strength
And makes my spirit whole.

A way that's built through God/man Christ,
The one that paved the road,
For on a cross he died for me
And took my heavy load.

Then he again in life
Put death as option's loss,
And in a risen conquering voice,
He pointed toward the cross.

He conquered death and all man's sin
By rising from the grave.
He died to pay the price for sin
That he mankind could save.

A way of life, of hopes, of dreams
Built full and made complete.
Until that day the sky will part
And all who love him meet.

I Am

"I am that I am," said the Lord of Hosts.
I am that I am beyond anyone's boast.

I am to mankind the leader of ways.
I am to life the keeper of days.

I am that I am the Spirit of souls.
I am the creator that makes one whole.

I am the beginning and I am the end.
I am the power that leadership sends.

I am the grace with provisions exist.
I am with patience when people resist.

I am with judgement when justice shall reign.
I am the Redeemer who is coming again.

I am the one who is waiting for you.
I am the omniscience in all that you do.

I am your Savior and since man's fall,
I Am has been waiting to answer your call.

Entitlement

Protests in the street,
Speeches in the square,
"Give us what we want," they say,
"For what you think, we do not care."

The prize in life is lots more stuff,
Stuff we get for free.
We do not care who pays the price
As long as it's for me.

How long this lasts, it all depends
On who we get to pay the bill.
We're taking all that we can get.
All other thoughts are only swill.

How free is freedom's plain to act
On churning open seas or across an open field?
When you sow the seed of self and self alone,
You'll bear the harvest of an empty yield.

Beware you traveler of want,
You who triangulates your grasp of life.
For in putting aside the future for the now,
You build a hopeless platform filled with strife.

A Passing Phase

We look at life and all its ways
And see the depths of passing days.
We laugh and weep; we work and sleep,
And hope for best in every craze.

We walk the miles and climb the hills
With all the bumps and turns.
We drink the milk of many clowns
And follow many yearns.

We really live our life alone
When only for ourselves,
We often spurn the love of those
Who help us use what's on our shelves.

We wade through all the twists and spins
And check each crevice for a fault.
We kick the dust along the trail,
Shaping time and gifts to cult.

We never cease to capture
Every twirling wind and way.
We finally come to rest when life runs out
And all goes back to basic clay.

There are the laughers, the criers, and kneelers. There are probably a million other passing phases that we encounter in a lifetime. The greatest phases are those that draw us close to God.

The Hope of Humankind

The conquered and the conquerors
Move down the battlefields of time,
With the rhythm and the chaos
Of a mountain's well-fought climb.

The anxious revolution
That plots the world's own plight,
Will never give to changing
Apart from pain and fight.

But lo, he comes, the one placed man
From God in time's own way.
To bring to revolution's thought
A path of hope for a brighter day.

He comes in humble means,
His method maimed by man,
Whose selfish heart and legal bent
Makes heartless love's demand.

Then faltered moment bent to dim
That hope upon the cross,
When scattered friend and committed hearts
Feel then that all is lost

But as the darkest part of night
Comes just before the dawn,
His death was just a prelude
To the work that God has done.

For in life he changes lives of people
With a revolution bathed in love.
For Christ is the greatest hope of man
And points us all to heaven above.

For the Joy

Most of us feel that joy
Is birthed in the comfort zone of life.
A place where the celebration of ecstasy reigns
And life is experiencing its most buoyant moment.
But joy is not birthed in celebration,
Rather in the crucible of fire and testing.

When the crushing possibility of defeat
Demands that we run the gauntlet
Of patience, pain, and adversity,
We find the final outcome of truth upon our lives
As a forged ingot of pureness in accomplished love;
And along the road of divine purpose,
We find joy.

Joy comes as God would have it come,
Not through frivolous fervor or shallow, superficial
thought,
But through timely testing, toil, and trust.
It's not decided by the board of directors
Or inherited in the genes.
It is not passed down through tradition
Or recreated by events of ritual
That have long since lost their reality.

Joy comes at the end of long nights of faithfulness
By people who desire
To put all things created together at the right time,
At the right place,
And for the right reasons.
In the end they experience one of God's greatest gifts,
Joy, that fills the heart forever.

Thoughts on the Past

I ambled down a cobwebbed hall
All spent with age and endless time.
I pondered thoughts of sentiment
And caught a glimpse of history's chime.

The air is stale from store of dust
That tells the days that lie in wait
To bring another age to bear upon
The past of bygone trait.

It's gone, the paths that time has walked
And passive hauntingly it looks.
I find its stare from past man's flair
Has given its heritage to books.

Sinking Sails

Look behind you to the wake of your life.
Think of your life as a ship on the sea.
Look at your journey and how far you have come
From the shore where the moor used to be.

Am I powered, or at sail, or am I adrift
And channeled out into the deep?
Do I know what to do when the day grows dim
Or my boat begins to seep?

What am I trusting to guide me to shore,
To the safety of harbor's care?
A buoy, or a star, or the God up above
With the guidance to get me there?

On Faith in Doing

Decision at the crossroads of life
Brings me always to a point of despair.
For I must always reach beyond myself
To something more that's there.

My progress dims when put to the test
Upon the path of life.
Until I pass that constant point where
Faith wins over strife.

Oh how I fight with pride and wit
With a battle's dust and din,
Until at last the light breaks through
And faith comes forth to win.

It's always there and has always been
A mustard seed or more
To slaves and servants as they serve
And draw upon their store.

To all are given the able right
To a grain of two or three,
For putting faith to the martyr's test
Brings all God's best to me.

Seeking and Finding

There must be a place
Where the goals are complete.
There must be a hope beyond mind.
There must be a life
Through which life can be found
With an end only faith can find.

There must be a God,
Yes a God great and bold,
Whose strength never quite is revealed,
With infinite grace
And personal love,
Through man's unbelief is concealed.

But try him by faith,
Reach out lonely hand
And the secret is told past the veil.
His Spirit and strength
Fills the life of a soul
Like the wind that fills a sail.

Seeking Love

A fervent, factual, faithful prayer
Was sent aloft to heaven.
I wonder if the God above
Will see an answer given.

As guiding grace moves into place
The answer from above.
My heart is filled with awesome peace
And the solace of God's love.

The struggle with an earnest thought
That flies upward from our heart
Can never find a quiet place
Without a God who does his part.

A part that's built with all expanse,
A part that transcends time,
A part that takes eternity
And makes its virtues mine.

A part that finally makes complete
A lasting perfect peace.
A part that shares agape love
And gives my soul release.

Talking Through

They talked about the hand of God.
They talked about his care.
They talked about believing faith
And life so bright and fair.

They talked about the price for sin.
They talked about his love.
They talked about a higher place
And even heaven's dove.

They talked about the trials of pain.
They talked about their needs.
They talked about a God of gifts
Without a God who does his part.

They talked along into the night,
They talked away the hours.
They talked and never did a thing
For fruit and growing flowers.

The talking finally ended
Of the Christian's strength and brawn.
They never touched an outside soul
For the time had come and gone.

Chosen Opportunity

I glanced at the sky.
The sun shines bright.
How much can I do
Before the night?

I leaned on a post
And thought about life;
The love and the stress,
The kids and the wife.

For a moment I'm gripped
With a feeling of fear.
What leans on me?
Who knows I'm here?

A bird falls dead.
A truck stops short.
The insistent get
Their day in court.

But to life, the sky,
The work to be done,
My God moves me on
As his chosen son.

On Being

May God help me
When I disagree
To keep on being
What a brother should be.

When I feel the tension
And pain of a rift,
May I search for an answer
Not set us adrift.

May I get to the heart
Of whatever it be
That keeps us from seeing
What our eyes should see.

May I walk on the road
That my brother has trod,
Seeking to bring us together
As brothers with God.

May I finally confront
The issues at hand
And tear down the walls
Of culture's demands.

Real Life

The role and real of life,
The yes and then the no;
The good, the better, and the best.
Of which is one to show?

Struggle for maturity,
But don't you dare grow old.
The finest things in life you see
Are bought but never sold.

They're bought with purpose, pain, and toil
On the battlefield of life.
They come with effort, thought, and zeal,
And many times with strife.

They're built with building blocks of love,
Of patience and with care.
They rest in strength of hopeful hearts
Fulfilled and always there.

So build and buy, think hard, grow strong;
Plan with an end in sight,
Then dream great dreams with the stars
That shine brightest in the darkest night.

Moving and Free

I looked at a rosebud
The first one of spring;
I thought of the beauty
Its presence would bring.

I stared at a wall.
The stones seemed to say,
Be strong and courageous
As you follow life's way.

I looked in the mirror
And there I saw me.
I wondered why life
Has made me so free.

The rosebud will rise
And shortly will fall.
The stones never move
As they're fixed in the wall.

But I am a soul
So free to move on,
By grace I'll be here
When the rose will be gone.

The Faithful Call

There's a call that comes to the faithful
Who have given their hearts to the Lord.
It's a call that commands our commitment
To the message of his Word.

There's a light that is our reflection
That shines from our Savior above.
In him we find our redemption
And we live as agents of love.

Accept Jesus today as your Savior.
Give your heart to the Savior on high.
Don't let the pleasures of this present world
Keep heaven from passing you by.

In his life-giving power we stand
Serving Jesus every day.
And as examples of Christ's work
We sow his love along life's way.

The Solemn Moment

Why is the world so full of noise?
The cacophony of sound engulfs our being.
The wall of conflicting sounds makes it
Almost impossible to hear the searching of the human
heart.

Where is the quiet place where the human spirit
Can reach out and touch the hand of God?

I went to church the other day.
There was so much said and sung so loudly,
My brain became distracted from the message.
My mind drifted into analyzing the whole of the
presentation.

That might not be the right place to land,
But it is an honest place.
On the other hand, as I looked around me,
I saw others caught up in the moment.

There was the beat of the drums,
The strumming of the guitars,
The swaying of the singers who were into the rhythms
and repetition of the modern beat.

But I cannot judge what God was doing for others,
only observe what he was doing for me at the time.

My wandering mind drifted toward wondering
Whether they were trying to humanly
Create a presence of God in the sanctuary.
It came across to me sort of like people trying to
Rub two sticks together to make a fire,
Or dancing around a pagan fire to create rain.

I was there; I was certainly a part,
But of which part, I wonder.
I really wanted to find a quiet spot
To seek in a corporate setting of assembly.
The enlarged presence of God resonating
In my heart the promise of "For where two or three
Gather in my name, there am I with them."

I so desired to look into the midst

And experience some essence of Shekhinah glory.

To recharge my heart with power

To keep overcoming the temptations of the world
system

And the pressure it puts on me,

As I pursue a life of personal faith

Centered on the promises of God.

Proverbs 3:5–6

Completion
Contemplation

As leaves drift down from waning trees
Upon a windswept road.
As wagons full of harvest fruit
Carry home the load.

It's time to check the measure of success
Against the effort of the day,
To stop and contemplate the course
Adjusting step-by-step the way.

The path that we have chosen,
The trails that we have walked,
The trip through life that's shaped our course
And every moment we have clocked.

Edging closer to our goals
By mountains climbed and oceans crossed,
May our treasures be in heaven stored,
Forever gained and never lost.

Of Night and Day

The sun goes down.
The lights come on
To counteract the failing day.
The streets grow dark
And doors go closed,
And night seems here to stay.

It ambles down
The dimming ways
That once were full of light.
And feeling knows
With darkness here,
The day has turned to night.

Come night, but go,
Move swiftly by.
Make dark the sky
As I sleeping lie.
But when I awake,
Be gone with you,
For we of the day
Have things to do.

The Observer

A centurion still stands today
Beside the cross in the crowded way
And waits for the times' revealed events
And what they'll have to say.

He waits to see kind acts of love,
He waits to view the pain,
He waits to do his part in life
To help the world to see again.

He might await for you and me
To bring our lives to bear,
For each of us to bear our cross
Releases him to do his share.

The Happy Band

Clipped, cleaned, and cloistered,
They gathered round their fire,
A happy band of brothers,
Whose efforts never tire.

They've put it all together
And stuffed God in a box,
And now they've banned forever
Their world of paradox.

Dependence

Learn to live for Jesus every day.
Learn to let his Word show you the way.
Learn to let his Spirit guide your life
And give you proper words to say.

Learn to stop and rest upon his strength.
Consider all of life—its height, and breadth, and
length.

Know that you alone can never make heaven's goal,
For it's only through righteousness of Christ
That we can comprehend the whole.

When I rest in him, I place my life in sacred trust.
I so transcend the fact that I am dust.

And when I lie in life's deep repose,
I need not fret, for I know the God who knows.

Winter Storm

When the wind blows jolly,
The frost is on the holly,
And the ice hangs low upon the eves.

When the winter keeps on blow-in',
The weather keeps on snow-in',
And every summer leaf has left the tree.

When we look through frosty panes
Upon the distant plains,
And we snuggle in until the storm has passed,

We discover life anew
As we seek out things to do,
But we're thankful when the storm is gone at last.

A Fleeting Summer Thought

It must be tough
When on Labor Day
So many friends
Go driving away.

Back to the places
They've come from afar.
Some go by train
And others by car.

Then comes the fall,
Winter, and spring,
There's Christmas and Easter,
Which happiness bring.

And with flowery burst
Of next summer's air,
The season has come
And your friends are back here.

History

History is the theater of experiences past,
Written in the annals of time.
History is the memory bank for the future,
Recording the absurd and savoring the sublime.

History is the fulcrum of hope,
Waving us past this present cope.
History is the accumulation of stuff,
Until at last the sovereign says enough.

History is here to stay.
No matter what we do, it will not go away,
Nor should it!

For as we speed along
The path toward heaven's gate,
We know with history lingering at our back,
It's never then ... but now ... that makes us late.

New York

New York, the city of dreams,
A place at the center of the world.
New York, the address
Where people come to get ahead in life,
Remain anonymous, or get their names up in lights.

New York, where people work a lifetime
And still have a long way to go.
New York, like a bucket of water
Is full of brimming delight.
Jump in and be the best swimmer,
Keeping pace both day and night.
Splash in the opportunity
And plunge to the depths of its core.
Leave and you'll find that it returns
Much the same as it was before.

New York is beckoning to you—
The best, the least and the lost.
New York calls for the world to come
No matter what the cost.
Come to the bustle and wave to the crowd.
Come blow your horn, for the whole city is loud.

The height of the buildings, the length of the blocks,
You can make it in college, or the school of hard
knocks.
Up from the bottom, the climb to the top
Will take you to midnight and never will stop.

On to the future with no thought of the past,
Churn out in your passion the die that you cast.
This is the place, the place you should be.
You'll never forget what you experience and see.

Circle of Time

Forever is a long way back,
When you think of how quick the day,
From morning till night seems but a flash,
Too short to show the way.

Forever is a long way back,
With the talents I have to show,
For when putting my best to the acid test,
I know there's a long way to go.

Forever is a long way back,
Though spending with careful thought,
The inflated charge of this mortal life
Costs me far much more than I've got.

Forever is a long way back,
A journey far into the night.
I wonder whose ship I should board
That will make that journey right.

Forever is a long way back,
Since humankind turned its course from grace
To death and despair and the dust of the earth,
When it fell from its heavenly place.

Forever is a long way back,
Will I make it alone if I try?
Forever lies long beyond even the strong,
And its truth hides deep in the sky.

But the journey begun with the single step,
Is a love-filled, hopeful, faithful event,
When given to God and his infinite love.
By faith, man will know where he's sent.

About Dan

What can I say about Dan?
If you're looking for advice, he's the man.
Whisking through the village on his bike he flies,
While waving kindly to the passerby.

Dan is attentive as he leads the way,
Serving Christ in his life each day.
Taking notes during every talk,
Dan is the man who walks the walk.

Leading and serving his presence we feel,
Because in Dan we know that his experience is real.
Staying the course of hope and love,
We know that Dan draws his strength from above.

So on his birthday so near the town's fountain,
Like Caleb of old … God give him his mountain.
For Dan will be faithful to climb to the top,
Inspiring us all to never stop.

From this day forward with seed in the ground,
Let's join with Dan and let faith abound.
Serving each day with a passionate call,
Let Dan's great spirit inspire us all.

From morning till night, here at home or abroad,
Keep planting the seed in the spiritual sod.
For surely as night will follow the day,
Dan's reflection of Christ will show us the way.

Watching and Waiting

I sit at the table and watch the impact
Of the breeze upon the trees;
Trees stripped of leaves that have fallen
As a result of the fall's retreat into winter.

I ponder the depth of winter when falling temperatures
Bring the frost and turn the grass to brown
And the cold turns rain to snow. How long will the
Snow last and the cold permeate the soil?

All of this is just a part of pondering thought,
As I look at life through the prism
Of my hopes and dreams.

Where we live determines
How much snow we will have.
And what we love affects
Whether we want to live there or not.

There are so many elements that impact our lives—
Our family, our work, our economic capacity,
Our preferences, our education, our house needs.
They all influence our decisions in life.

So as I sit at the table today watching and waiting
For what's next in life,
I also need to be thinking about how to use
The rest of my life in such a way as to assure
The next generation that life means more
Than just the pondering
Of today in this punctiliar moment.

Shine Forth to the Glory

The miracle of redemption
Sent to us from heaven above
Calls out to people of the world
To the saving grace of Christ's great love.

Refrain
Shine forth to the glory of the Lord.
Sing to the power of his Word,
Take the gospel to the world
As we go and give and pray.
Shine forth as we serve him every day.

Let the saints rise up with joy
As God leads us in the way
Be a lighthouse on the shore
As people witness what you say.

Shine forth to the glory of the Lord.
Sing to the power of his Word,
Take the gospel to the world
As we go and give and pray.
Shine forth as we serve him every day.

Be you reconciled to God
To the Father through the Son
Come by faith to Christ the Savior.
Let redemption's work be done.

Shine forth to the glory of the Lord.
Sing to the power of his Word,
Take the gospel to the world
As we go and give and pray.
Shine forth as we serve him every day.

God's Place for You

There's a place in the family of God
For all who believe in his Word.
There's a place in the family of God for those
Who accept Jesus Christ as their Lord.

Come to the fountain of life.
Come to the Son from above.
Come give your life to the Savior.
Come and experience his love.

There's a place in the body for you.
There's a guide who will show you the way.
There's a fullness of peace in his promises
That will give you strength for each day.

Refrain
There's a place of service for you,
For Christ has made you anew.
Receive of his grace as you run life's race,
For he's with you in all that you do.

Stop and Ponder

Alone along the silent shore,
Seeking waters calm with placid peace,
I am led to quiet thought
And its essence for release.

Be still my friend, be still.
We're children of the day
Just stop for a blissful moment
As you run along the way.

Stop and contemplate the hour
By the pond of purposed rest
Look around at nature's beauty
Give life to God and then be blest.

When We Say Goodbye

When we say goodbye
And prepare to part our ways,
Give thanks for the memories.

When we get up to go
And take leave of this day's show,
Give thanks for the memories.

When the laughter has ended
And we head for the doors,
Give thanks for the memories

When the applause stops
And silence fills the room,
Give thanks for the memories.

Be sure to take them home.
Reflect on them with love.
Add them to your special thoughts.
Store them in your heart.

Laugh and learn, talk and remember.
Share the joy and even shed a tear.
Open up your world of hope.
Learn to love and never fear.

Then stop!
Give thanks for the memories.

What's That, Mommy

What's that, Mommy? Oh, honey, that's a church. What does it do? It is a place where people come and are told about God. Who is God? God is hard to explain.

But who is God? God means many things to many people. If God has meaning, then what does God mean to us? God is nothing to us, because we don't believe in God.

We don't? Why? Well, because we can't see God, we believe he probably doesn't exist. Does that mean there is no God? Well, not exactly. Then why wouldn't we explore God and find out if he is real? Well, sometimes people do things in the name of God that we don't like. Well, that would mean we would be getting involved in religion.

What is religion? Religion is really about people expressing what they feel about God. What do we feel about God? Well, we really try not to feel anything about God because we don't think that God exists.

Why doesn't God exist? We believe that God is something that people make up to escape from real life. We don't need anything but ourselves, and that is

what is real. What makes real life real? People
learning to love each other as I love you.

Where does love come from? Love comes from the
way we feel about each other. If life is so perfect
without God, then why do people not love perfectly?

We need to work harder at it. Does love come from
work or work come from love?

There's something about life that draws us to love.
Could that something have anything to do with God?
Not if God doesn't exist. Then why do people build
the church and why do people want to love? Because it
is in our nature to do such things.

Is nature like being a tree? Not really. A tree is a plant
and we are animals. Are we like a cow or a horse? Sort
of, but we have the power to reason, which is more
than other animals have.

Mommy, can I reason that maybe there is a God?
Well, I guess if that's what you want to decide to do. I
think that's what I'd like to decide, because I don't
want to be alone. You have me and I will not leave
you alone.

If you die, I will be alone, but if I believe in God, I
will never be alone. Even if he doesn't exist, he will
make me feel I belong to something bigger than
myself. I might even think about Jesus and what he has
to offer.

Can we buy an ice cream cone now?

Another Look

All the lonely people
That make up the human race,
Each one as a person,
And each with one's own face.

A sea of lonely faces,
Each behind a mask,
Deciding how to reach each one
Is a burdened, heavy task.

A life laid down for human cause
Is hardly worth one's while,
Unless one finds the God-sent strength
To walk that extra mile.

Walking in Love

As you walk down the road of life
Filled with wonder, fear, and strife,
Hold hands in love with people dear.
Hug them close and keep them near.

We never know how long things last,
So savor the moment and remember the past,
So lift your sights above the fray,
And love your way through every day.

Thank You, Jesus

Thank you, Jesus. I know you're there
Looking down with tender care.
When I lift my heart in prayer,
Thank you, Jesus, I know you're there.

Come upon us, Lord, we pray,
Show us now your perfect way.
May thy Spirit make us see
How to live our lives in thee.

Expressing Love

The moment you loved me,
I knew it was real.
The touch of your hand
Gave me a thrill.

I looked in your eyes.
They expressed such great care.
I savored the moment
And was glad to be there.

It's been quite a journey
From that first day till now.
It's still at the feet
Of our love that I bow.

As God has provided
For each step of the way.
I stop and give thanks
For your love each day.

Living Circumstance

As we pass this place along the road of life
Where we've never been before,
It's in this moment of circumstance
That we stand before an open door.
We cannot always make the context,
Nor can we claim the cause,
But we must always rise above the fray,
Even when we pause.

Always test the victory
When the battle fought is won.
We dare not fail beyond the pale,
For the war is never done.
We travel on throughout the night
Seeking for the light of day.
We struggle with each moment
As we walk each step the way.

There is nothing there but reasoning hope
To fuel our moving on,
Each present moment shaping every moment past
To build our dreams upon.
Someday, somewhere, sometime
Invested through the days of toil,

We'll find at last the golden shore
For which we've sailed
And pray our planted flag of trust
Has been in God's most fertile soil.

ABOUT THE AUTHOR

Born in New Castle, Pennsylvania, Charles grew up in a Christian family. After high school he attended Nyack College (BSM), Manhattan School of Music (MM), continued his theological studies at Luther Rice Seminary, and became an ordained Baptist minister.

Charles has been married to Ethel Rigby for over sixty years. They have three adult children, Cynthia, Scott, and Mark; and four grandchildren, Alexander, Jessica, Oscar, and Erika. Charles and his wife began their ministry in New York City in 1955. They have served a number of Christian institutions and pastorates. During the last fifty-five years, Charles has served the Lord both in pastoral roles and in evangelism as executive director of Metropolitan Youth for Christ and the New York Bible Society. He is a pastor, writer, artist, musician, speaker, teacher, and administrator.

Charles is an author of many tracts, pamphlets, and a book entitled *More Than Volunteers*. Although retired, he teaches a seminar series on helping Christians find their place in the body life of the church, teaching Christians that their commitment to Christ empowers them to be more than volunteers.

CONTACT CHARLES RIGBY

E-MAIL: chucksrigby@gmail.com

CAN YOU HELP?

REVIEWS ARE EVERYTHING TO AN AUTHOR, BECAUSE THEY MEAN A BOOK IS GIVEN MORE VISIBILITY. IF YOU ENJOYED THIS BOOK, PLEASE REVIEW IT ON AMAZON AND OTHER BOOK REVIEWS SITES AND TELL YOUR FRIENDS ABOUT IT. THANK YOU!

OTHER BOOKS BY CHARLES

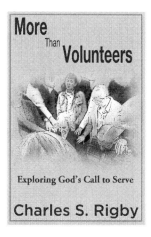

More Than Volunteers is a book dedicated to building better models of relationships between the institutional church and the people in the pews. The local church is always calling for volunteers, but in reality, it often fails creatively to define and equip the saints for the work of the ministry. This book leads the way for inspiring your church toward greater growth and understanding as a body of believers. Available on Amazon in softback and in Kindle eBook format.

www.amazon.com/More-Than-Volunteers-Exploring-Serve/dp/1936927047

93189598R00080

Made in the USA
Columbia, SC
09 April 2018